THE ART OF SAYING GOODBYE

the ART of Saying GOODBYE

How to Survive the Loss of a Love

ARTHUR SAMUELS, M.D.

Element
An Imprint of HarperCollins*Publishers*
77–85 Fulham Palace Road,
Hammersmith, London W6 8JB

The website address is: www.thorsonselement.com

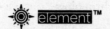

and *Element* are trademarks of
HarperCollins*Publishers* Ltd

First published 2000
This edition published 2003

1 3 5 7 9 10 8 6 4 2

A catalogue record for this book
is available from the British Library

Cover design by Kathryn Sky-Peck

ISBN 0 00 716512 9

Printed and bound in Great Britain by
Clays Ltd, St Ives plc

This book is not intended to replace the services of a physician, therapist
or counselor. Any application of the recommendations set forth in the
following pages is at the reader's discretion. The reader should consult with
a qualified professional concerning the recommendations in this book.

DEDICATION

This book is dedicated to Ruth Steinman Samuels, Ph.D. in Anthropology and Doctor of Jurisprudence, who passed on four days ago. Ruth, I can hear your laugh as you make some cosmic joke about my reference to your scholarship. I can also feel your compassion at my tears as I write this. You were a dedicated scholar, but even deeper was your dedication to wifehood and motherhood. Your breath was short and each word a precious pearl in those last few hours. When I told you I was dedicating this book to you, you made no comment. There were far more pressing things for you to share with me and all those who were touching you with their love at your bedside.

I remember our first brief separation before we were engaged fifty years ago. I thought I had lost you to an old boyfriend. I had never felt such despair! It led to fierce determination to win you back. There were many separations since, all painful. But all resulting in greater independence and ultimately a deeper love between us.

I sensed that you could feel the pure joy of my love as I sent the warmth of my hand to yours after your heart stopped beating. Did I imagine or did I really feel warmth coming back from your cold body? The physical reality doesn't matter. That warmth was a miracle to me just as much as the presence of the spirit of you all around me is, at this moment. I grieve that I cannot touch you or hear your voice. But there is no despair with both of us free from the intrusions of the pain of past misunderstandings and separations. I hear your message clearer and share loving feelings with you at a depth that I could never imagine before.

I also dedicate this book to you, dear reader. It comes with the prayer that it will help you avoid the folly of unnecessary separations and nurture you through the grief of the ultimate physical separation. May it guide you to the beautiful depth of love that transcends death.

ART SAMUELS

TABLE OF CONTENTS

Foreign Country • Cherishing Your Roots • Embracing Your New Country

HOW TO USE THIS BOOK

I honor you for your willingness to learn the *"Art of Saying Goodbye."* You are about to develop a valuable skill that will serve you well for the rest of your life: The ability to let go of someone or something that is precious to you and end up feeling richer than before your loss. This book tells you how to do this.

Read each paragraph slowly to give yourself the time to experience what personal meaning it has for you. Repeat the exercises over and over again whenever you have a painful emotion. You will find them progressively easier to do. The duration of gritful discomfort will become briefer and the resulting pearls more beautiful.

The pain of loss often returns on important anniversaries. It also can be brought on by special sounds, songs, fragrances, and sights. Each one is an occasion for using the techniques you will learn. To honor what is past and to strengthen yourself in the present moment.

Each time you re-read the book you will learn something new about yourself and your relationships. It will be helpful to read it at times when you're not experiencing losses. You will discover this to be a life-affirming experience that grows more precious with the years.

INTRODUCTION

Grief can be a measure of how well you have lived and how deeply you have loved.

Grief then serves as a beacon of light showing you the new way to rich learning.

This book will teach you how to love yourself through the excruciating pain of losing a loved one, whether through death or separation. You will also learn to take care of grief resulting from other losses—loss of a job, status, money, moving away from home, etc.

You will learn how to use the experience as a rite of passage to help you fill the void.

You will discover how to make grief your ally, an ally that enables you to transform feelings of helplessness into strong new parts of yourself.

You will discover how to keep the spirit of the one you have lost alive in your heart forever. The most cherished part of them becomes a growing part of you.

The experience of the joy of your closeness to them transcends death. The heartbeat of your emerging new self is a victory bell celebrating your love for the one who has "died."

These same concepts may be applied to help you with any losses. Chapter 15 illustrates the use of creative grieving in divorce or separation from a long-term lover or friend.

Chapter 13 teaches you how to handle other major losses. The loss of money or other material things, the pain of moving away from a familiar place, and the loss of status produce grief that is endemic in our rapidly changing society.

Everything in life is impermanent. It is essential to be able to adapt to this reality, particularly now, when changes are occurring with ever-increasing rapidity.

Clinging to people or to things in a universe that is, by definition, impermanent causes pain. You become lost in the past and fearful of the future.

Practicing the creative grieving procedures enables you to stay in an enriched present—the only time you can really experience the reality of your full aliveness.

IT FEELS LIKE I'M
DROWNING!

Many years ago, my wife and I were walking along a beautiful beach in Mexico. It lined a small bay going out to the Caribbean Sea. We looked out toward the horizon and were enraptured by the sight of the gently undulating waves coming into the mouth of the bay. We decided to swim there in order to be closer to its beauty.

Both good swimmers, we set out at a leisurely pace. The distance was deceiving. It was much further to the mouth of the bay than it appeared to be on land. We paused, trying to decide whether to swim on or return to the beach. We were not tired, but we were getting a little anxious about being so far out.

Suddenly we were caught in a powerful riptide. I found myself carried helplessly head over heels by the relentless waves. I had glimpses of huge fish deep down in the water. Back at the surface, I became frightened. Where is Ruthie? I saw her frantically thrashing in the water nearby. I somehow managed to force my way to her through the surf. She screamed "We're going to drown!" Being habitually oppositional, I calmed my own terror by saying very firmly "Relax!

We will stay close to each other and move with the tide. Don't fight it. Just float with it." My fear eased even as I spoke to her. Her fear diminished as we began moving with the tide instead of fighting it. The feeling of terrifying helplessness had disappeared. I was still anxious. I didn't know how this would end, but neither of us was drowning.

After a few minutes, which felt like an eternity, the tide eased and we were able to slowly swim back to shore. As we lay exhausted on the beach, we were surprised to find it deserted. We could have drowned. There was no one there who could have saved us. We had been totally alone in our adventure.

As I write this story, I find my chest tightening. New grief over Ruth's recent death is welling up around the memory of our survival. I start to push it down but then breathe into the tightness and let the tears flow. They are saying, "I will always miss you, my beloved. It hurts to be without you." As the tears roll down my cheeks, I feel the pain turning into a deep, peaceful feeling. I can see her smiling at me, and I can almost hear her special chuckle. I feel her spirit inside of me helping me to write all of this down. The process of living is good—grief and all!

We naturally try to run away from pain. The more we

fight the inevitable reality of loss, the more punishing the discomfort becomes. Struggling against the strong current can drown us in chronic depression. Touching the pain with love and flowing with it carries us to inner peace.

Our tears are a healing balm. We can cry as long as we need to. We might fear that we will never stop crying, but if they are really tears of goodbye, they, like other emotions, have a beginning and an end. When we breathe into that part of our body where the suffering appears to be located (commonly the chest, eyes, or throat), after a moment of apparent greater pain, we can let it flow freely. Although it may be hard for you to believe at this moment, true grief carries us ultimately to inner peace.

"THE REAL YOU"

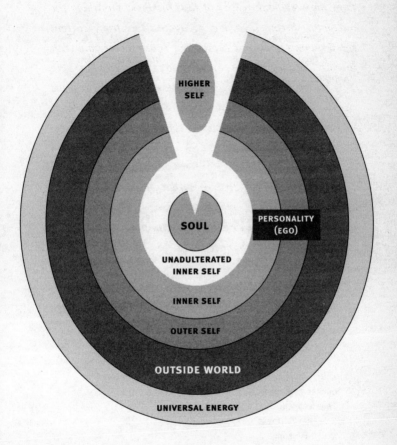

HIGHER
SELF

SOUL

PERSONALITY
(EGO)

UNADULTERATED
INNER SELF

INNER SELF

OUTER SELF

OUTSIDE WORLD

UNIVERSAL ENERGY

TABLE A

Qualities Present in
the Core Self
(Soul, God Within, Buddha
Self, Universal Energy)

Compassionate
Loving
Wise
Receptive
Allowing
Unlimited
Intuitive
Sense of oneness with
other people
Sense of inner strength
Total aliveness
Mindful
Spontaneous
Creative
Inspired
Peaceful
Open
Connected
Touches present Reality
Oneness with Nature
Outer Softness
Evolving
Humble

TABLE B

Characteristics of the
Inner/Outer Self
(Ego)

Judgmental
Fearful
Opinionated
Intrusive
Dominating
Limited
Rationalizing
Seeks fixed position
Clinging
Controlled
Restrictive/reactive
Conventional
Anxious
Defensive
Separated
Identity seeking
Stresses differences
Nature ignored

GOOD GRIEF!

*Grief has many positive aspects to it. Let's take
a look at some of them before we delve
into the grieving process.*

BADGE OF SUCCESS

The tears you shed are medals of honor. Each one bears a brave message of caring. It says that you have the courage to love and the courage to let go. It can be an indication of how well you have loved. If this is true of you, you have earned your Ph.D. in loving.

You have lost a major object of your love,
but you can never lose your ability to love.

RITE OF PASSAGE

In many cultures, an initiation ceremony is performed marking the passage from one life phase to another. This ceremony is sometimes physically painful or requires many hours of preparation. Young Jewish boys or girls may spend years learning difficult ancient teachings and an entire new language (Hebrew) in preparation for their bar mitzvah or bat mitzvah. The discipline required to learn all of this is the same discipline that is required to lead a successful adult life. The ceremony marks a proud passage into adulthood. Similarly, grief and mourning may be regarded as a rite of passage or transition from one phase of life to a wiser, more mature phase. Until you have had the courage to go through the pain of separation, you tend to cling to the past. When you successfully move through grief, you become stronger. It is as if you had been brittle iron going through fire to become tougher, more resilient steel.

CREATING A NEW SELF

The creative grieving technique teaches you to internalize the positive attributes of the one you have lost. Experiencing these important character traits inside yourself frees you to be a fuller, more creative and adventurous person.

OPPORTUNITY FOR
A NEW LIFE

I f you stay sad about the moon, you'll miss the rising sun.

Grief passes, and with it goes a major part of your way of relating in the world that occupied much of your time and energy. You are free now to encounter the world in a fresh new way. For instance, if you can no longer be a daughter to your mother, now you can empower yourself to become a mother to yourself and others. Changes in yourself, the way you can use your energy, and your attitude toward your own fulfillment and place in the world open the door to vast new possibilities.

HONORING YOUR
ANCESTORS

H onoring your ancestors and other lost loved ones begins in your heart and soul. There are many external ways to honor your ancestors and loved ones. In many Asian cultures, homes contain an altar with pictures of family members who have died. Their presence is recognized and included in daily life. Ancestors are kept up to date on all important family events and are consulted for advice. This nurtures the continuity of the family. This ancient ritual may not bring solace to you, yet there is great value in creating your own ways to honor the presence of your ancestors and deceased loved ones and to include them in your daily life.

Facets of the personality of the deceased live on in you. You create a place in your life that mirrors the place in your heart. What better way to honor your ancestors? The place where you feel loss is the same place you can consciously fill with the inspiration your love carried for your loved ones. By honoring your own feelings, both of loss and of joy in memory of your beloved, you can heal the rupture caused by death.

It is in the living of your life with the continuity of love,
not lost but transformed, that you honor yourself
and your loved ones.

THE FIVE JEWELS
OF GRIEVING

By surviving a major loss and grieving creatively, you are fortified against the fear of further losses. Your life is enriched by three great new potential strengths:

1

Increased ability to live with impermanence

Nothing in life is permanent. Surviving a major loss and grieving creatively strengthens your ability to live life fully through its ups and downs.

2

Increased capacity to take on new challenges

Knowing that you can survive makes the anticipated pain of possible failure less of a threat. This frees you to enjoy your creativity.

3

Increased wisdom

Since death illuminates the preciousness of life, you can now see more clearly what is most important to you and live your life accordingly.

4

Increased maturity

When you take care of yourself as you grieve, you remain open to others but less dependent upon them.

5

Increased capacity to relate closely to others

Although you might be initially fearful, you will ultimately be less afraid to enter close relationships, because you now know that you can survive the loss of them.

2

THE DIFFERENCE
BETWEEN GRIEF
AND DEPRESSION

Grief is a painful and, oftentimes, overwhelming response to loss. It is a natural, healthy response to being separated from someone you love. In death, where the loss is permanent, you can feel as if you have lost a part of yourself. There is no healthy way of successfully avoiding the deep, sharp hurt you feel. Health comes in the expression of your true feelings. So welcome those healing tears you feel welling up inside of you, even though you might be afraid that you will never stop crying. The good news is that grief is time limited. You can use this book to learn ways to shorten your suffering and to use the experience to strengthen yourself.

Depression is usually avoidable. It is a duller, heavier feeling than grief. Depression is spread out over a longer period of time. It can occur with or without a real loss in your life. Depression can last a lifetime. The good news about depression is that it is treatable and preventable.

There are two common causes of depression associated with grief. One is the result of dysfunctional thinking patterns. For instance, if someone dies and you tell yourself, "I will never be happy again," you are compounding the fresh pain of grief by projecting it into the future. You are engaging in negative fortunetelling. You are also "generalizing" by saying, "Since I am unhappy now, I will always be unhappy."

Another source of depression comes from the habit of making yourself sad when something unwanted occurs. This represents the inner child saying, "I am going to stay sad until someone comes along and makes me feel better." In this instance, "I will stay sad until my loved one comes back."

Other causes of depression are poor diet, physical illness and a congenital predisposition to depression. All of these are medically treatable.

3

YOU HAVE ALL
IT TAKES TO
SEE IT THROUGH

While focusing on your pain during the grieving process, you may lose contact with aspects of yourself that are strong and affirming. These parts of your psychological self can help to nurture and heal the wounded part back to wholeness.

The diagram on page xvii illustrates the relationship between these different parts of yourself. Notice how small the segment labeled "ego" is. It is often the only part of ourselves we are familiar with. The ego is the "me" you are thinking about when you think of yourself. When you are grieving, your ego feels seriously damaged, vulnerable, and often helpless. It's habitual emotional and behavioral patterns are magnified (see Table B, page xviii). You are apt to become fearful as you try to cling to the past. You may vehemently judge yourself or others for what happened. You feel alienated from others and different from people who are not grieving. Your whole position in life has crumbled. In your attempt to reestablish a sense of certainty (which so often is undercut when a major loss is suffered), you may try to control others by bossing them around or by clinging to them. You might even feel as though you are going crazy, because the familiar source that you used to reinforce your identity is gone. All of these reactions compound the discomfort you are already feeling.

Outwardly, your ego expresses itself in the cloak of your personality. This part of you is firmly established early in childhood. As you feel grief, look at the diagram and note again what a small area that part of you that feels so demolished, occupies. The largest part of you, which we will be tapping into, remains undamaged and is a powerful source for healing.

THE INNER SELF

This is the part of your psychological self that suffers the most in terms of grief. Your inner self ranges in age from infancy to your present age. It is the heir to your childhood. When vulnerable, it is strongly influenced by memory traces from childhood. It may feel helpless, alone, and frightened, just as it felt when you were a small child being left alone. The trauma of your loss can push all of your energy back into that time and space when you actually could not survive without outside help. Your little self really believes, "I cannot go on without him/her."

THE OUTER SELF

This is the part of you that interacts with the outside world. It is modeled after your mother and father or other authorities you have come in contact with. It can be very loving and nurture your inner self through its anguish, or it can be harsh and critical and shame your inner self for hurting. If you have been self-confident and loving of yourself, that indicates that you have developed a self-supporting, loving outer self that will automatically comfort your inner self at this time.

On the other hand, if you have developed a self-critical outer self, it is even more difficult for your inner self to heal. Much of this book is aimed toward strengthening the loving potential of your outer self.

The outer self is constantly checking the outside world and monitoring the inner self accordingly. Unfortunately, it often is unable to be objective because it is looking through lenses that have been distorted by past experiences.

THE SOUL SELF

What I am referring to as the soul self is your unadulterated inner self. This aspect of the self has different names in different religions. The soul self might be called the Christ or the Buddha self. It is made up of universal energy or God energy. You are born with it, and it is unchangeable and lasts forever. Your soul self was there before your birth and will be there after you die. Rabbi Joshua Lieberman said, "We are all little pieces of God." Your soul self is your own very special piece of the Almighty, the anointed one, or universal energy. If you are not a follower of "organized religion," you might be more comfortable thinking of this divine part of yourself as a fluctuating, harmonic energy field. Your soul self is in total and complete harmony with the vast central energy field of the universe. It is a portion of time and space—the core "mystery" of scientific inquiry. This is what all things are made of, and this pure "nothingness" is everything at the same time. If you were looking into an electron microscope, the soul self's presence would be seen at the place where matter turns into energy and energy turns into matter.

When you experience it, you are engulfed in an aura of peaceful love and generative excitement that can best be described as blissful.

The soul self is represented in the diagram labeled "The Real You" (pages xvii–xviii) as your very center. It is the bull's eye that offers you all of the wonderful experiences listed in Table A when you touch it. Your soul self automatically and effortlessly connects you with your higher self and God self (universal energy).

THE GOD SELF OR UNIVERSAL ENERGY

This is the same material as the soul self. It is found everywhere—in all things and in all people. As Paul Tillich described God, "God is not a person, but not less than a person. God is the ground of being." It is the inevitable, miraculous energy of which all things are created. Since everything stems from it, we all have this bond in common. All people and all things are indeed children of the Creator. Knowing and feeling this produces natural love for the world around you and everything in it. After all, every detail in the universe, be it grand or minute, is your kin.

THE HIGHER SELF

Notice the pie slice labeled the "higher self" in the "Real You" diagram. It is connected to all the other parts of you. This aspect of the self is the center of mindful wisdom for both your inner and outer self. It is deeply connected with your individual soul self and with universal energy (or God). Because it remains uncontaminated, it actually comprises your only unobstructed, undistorted view of the outside world. It has an uncontaminated, nonjudgmental view of you. Your higher self is mindful, deeply compassionate, loving, and understanding. It is that part of you that gives you a sense of profound love. By tapping into the higher parts of yourself, you automatically experience the qualities listed in Table A. Watering these qualities by dwelling in the ever-available higher parts of yourself (as you will soon be learning to do), will enable you to transcend the withering aspects of grief.

You feel compassionate and loving toward yourself and others. You allow others to help you and are open to receive spiritual comforting. You feel closer to others. You sense inner peace and feel connected in a deep way with God as well as the one you have lost. Eventually, you feel inspired to create a new life for yourself.

4

WHO WILL TAKE
CARE OF ME?

The only emotions that do not change are those that you ignore. They lie like a pocket of infection deep inside your mind and body. Grief is particularly virulent if it is not drained.

You may feel it on the surface of your mind in the form of anxiety or restlessness, a painful itch that you cannot scratch. You try to run away from it by keeping busy, working all of the time, or getting lost in some addiction—alcohol, drugs, sex, or gambling. Nothing works. All emotions must be acknowledged with mindful, loving awareness.

Acknowledging grief, the most painful of emotions, is like the surgeon's scalpel opening a way out for the trapped infection. As you let the feelings drain out, healing occurs.

The next section teaches you a self-nurturing meditation that can help you through the various stages of grief.

NURTURING YOUR
INNER SELF

The loss of a loved one is a frightening experience. It can make you anxious about the future. Your inner self may be silently crying out, "Who will be there to love me? I am afraid to be alone."

Many of your childhood fears of abandonment are being reactivated in the memory traces of your mind. When this occurs, your inner self feels very small and helpless. It is important to take time out to tenderly take care of that part of yourself. What follows is a wonderful way of accomplishing that, at a deep psychological level, which will help to fill the emptiness inside and dispel fears in the future.

Current pain stimulates memory traces of past losses in the nervous system. They are buried within the cells of your body. Because of this, you feel exactly as you did as a small child. Therefore the pain of your present loss is compounded by pain experienced in the past.

Fortunately, although you may for a time feel as helpless as a child, you are not, in fact, helpless at all. Your outer self has years of survival skills that you can

call into play. It is your outer self that can begin nurturing your inner self through the stages of grief.

The following self-nurturing meditation is effective.
It may be the most important thing you learn in this
book. During this process, your outer self gives total
acceptance and love to your inner self. Taking a few
minutes to do this whenever you have unwanted emotions is sound practice for the rest of your life and can be
transforming!

MEDITATION ON THE INNER SELF

1

Remember having loving feelings toward someone or
something (a pet will be fine).

2

Focus on that loving feeling and breathe it into the center
of your chest. You might experience it as a "lightening-up"

or a tingling sensation. Perhaps you will feel warmth in that area. You might be able to perceive it as having a special color. Fill that part of your chest with loving energy. Remembering that there is a part of you capable of loving, is what is important here.

3

Locate where in your body the feeling of grief is most centered. Common places are the heart, stomach, or throat—but it can be anywhere or may be sensed in your whole body.

4

Imagine seeing, hearing, and touching the sad part of yourself.

You might "see" a sad expression on the image of that part of you, or it might appear as a vague sensation. That part may be any age, from infancy up to your present age. You might not see a clear image at all. You may only have a vague sensation of physical discomfort somewhere in your body.

5

Imagine holding that sad part of you in your arms tenderly.

Take a deep breath. Imagine opening the space around your heart and compassionately breathing in the painful feelings. Your outer self is now being a perfect mother or father, being mindful and totally accepting of the pain of your inner self.

6

As you breathe out, exhale love and compassion to your inner self.

Send that loving energy out with all of your heart.

7

Keep focused.

Forget the circumstances or the cause of the grief at this time. Your inner self needs your total care and attention. Simply keep breathing in the dark energy of sadness or grief and sending back the lighter energy of love and compassion.

You are using your body, mind, and soul to transform pain into love.

Keep doing this until you notice a change. It might be a change into another emotion—anger or fear, for example.

Continue breathing in the new emotion, accepting it totally and sending your inner self love and compassion.

Continue until you feel relief. This usually occurs in a few minutes if you stay focused.

If your mind wanders, it requires more time.

• If you have difficulty identifying specific emotions, imagine breathing in a dark, heavy energy and breathing out to the inner self a lighter, white energy.

• If you are unable to visualize your inner self, simply watch the physical sensation in your body that represents grief. Feel love and compassion for that painful feeling as you let it pass through you like waves rising and falling in the ocean.

MAKING ROOM FOR GOD

Now that your inner self is taken care of, you can contact your spiritual essence. Usually, thoughts and emotions fill your mind so that there is no space left in your awareness to feel the comfort of a divine presence.

If you follow the inner-self meditation with a meditation on your breath, your mind will be more open to God's presence.

1

When you feel peaceful, focus on your breath. Say to yourself as you breathe in, "I am breathing in." As you breathe out, say "I am breathing out." Drop your attention to your abdomen and watch it rise as you inhale and fall when you exhale.

2

Awareness of the breath gradually replaces other thoughts. You simply watch them and let them go by like a bird flying overhead. Then you return to your breathing.

3

Gradually let your focus rest on the quiet place at the end of the exhalation, before you breathe again.

Meditating on the breath of life, described in Chapter 14, facilitates this process and deepens the experience.

This silent place that is free of thought has been referred to as the "dwelling place of God" in many different religions.

4

Imagine the energy of the creator rising from the earth through the base of your spine and up through your spinal column as you inhale. Press the tip of your tongue to the roof of your mouth and roll your eyes toward the heavens. Pause a few seconds as you experience yourself filled with divine energy. Then exhale that holy spirit down into your body. Repeat this procedure a few times.

For many people, having these instructions on tape has been helpful. An extended version of this inner-self meditation read by the author is available via email at stresstc@accencom.net or by phoning 1-888-333-6402

5

Feel God's presence.

You are not alone.

Before, you felt lost in the void left by the death of your loved one.

Now feel God's presence.

The universal energy of God's love joins the loving parent part of you in filling the void.

Rest quietly. A divine presence soothes you.

If a familiar prayer comes to your awareness now, slowly savor the sweet depth of its meaning.

MORE WAYS OF NURTURING YOURSELF THROUGH GRIEF

The trauma of grief is a real one. You need as much support and caring as you would need after a major accident.

Taking Good Physical Care of Yourself

There are many studies that show that the onset of major physical illness is often related to recent losses. This occurs because your immune system is depressed by the shock. Taking care of yourself physically will make this turning point in your life easier to handle emotionally.

1

Be certain to eat a well-balanced diet. Increase your intake of vitamin C to 2000 mg. per day and double the usual dose of multivitamins for thirty days.

2

Decrease your work load. Your emotional work load will require much of your energy in the near future.

3

Be certain to get enough sleep. Using the self-nurturing

and creative grieving procedures will help calm you down.

Valerium and Melatonin are natural herbal sleep facilitators and are available in health food stores.

If all of these don't work, ask your physician for the least habit-forming sleeping medication available.

4

Exercise regularly, but not to the straining point.

5

Touch and be touched frequently. A heart-felt hug is the most healing of all.

Take long, warm bubble baths.

If you have a pet, talk to it and cuddle it.

If you don't have a pet and you live alone, get one as soon as possible. It is a safe, quick way of reactivating the loving part of yourself. Animals intuitively know how to love you back.

Taking Good Emotional Care of Yourself

1

Use the techniques offered in this book every time you feel bad (as often as a hundred times a day, if necessary, in the beginning).

With disciplined practice, these techniques can be effective in just a few minutes.

2

Ask for help and good company. You do not have to stay alone to prove you are strong.

At this time, it is much more appropriate to cry in somebody's arms.

3

Find something pleasant to do. For example, listen to music.

It is advisable to do things that are enjoyable as long as the joy is authentic and does not represent a running away from grief.

You might feel despair one minute and be laughing five minutes later.

Having fun does not mean you did not love the person who died.

If you feel grief during the activity, stop and take time out to nurture your inner self.

5

STAGES OF GRIEF

Adapted from Elizabeth Kübler Ross,
On Death and Dying *(New York: Macmillan, 1969)*

If you accept the pain of grief, you will soon find that it can become an ally. If you try to reject it, as will be discussed later, it can become a formidable enemy.

The sooner you accept your loss, the better it will be for you—but don't push it. According to your personality, you may go through any or all of the following stages as you face the pain and cleansing tears of really saying goodbye. They may come in any order:

1

Numbing Out

At first, all you may be feeling is numbness.

Accept that.

It is your nervous system's way of temporarily reducing the intensity of your pain so that your pain does not overwhelm you.

It is OK to go through the motions of your life without feeling emotions for a while.

This may last a few hours to a few weeks.

As soon as you begin to feel the pain, welcome it as a vital part of yourself.

Do not push it away by keeping busy.

Do not stifle the emerging cry with food.

Do not consciously attempt to ignore or numb your-self to it.

Emerging pain is a signal that you are beginning the "letting go" process.

2

Denial

You begin to feel your loss and then attempt to deny the reality of it.

"It's not true.

It's a mistake.

He/she has only gone away temporarily.

I won't believe it."

With denial, you might also try to isolate yourself from other people or situations that confront you with evidence that death has occurred.

Your inner self is trying to make believe that nothing bad has happened and your life will remain as it was before.

Let your compassion grow. Open space around your heart for that tender part of yourself that fears suffering. Accept the feeling of resistance. Soon the pain of your loss will seep in.

Hold that hurting part of you with love and compassion.

3

Anger and Guilt

"I hate myself for whatever I did to cause it or whatever I didn't do to prevent it.

I hate everyone.

Why should you feel good when I feel so bad?"

Your outer self is punishing your inner self.

Your inner self is beginning to face the real loss, and your outer self, instead of being comforting, is compounding the pain with "you should have" and "you are bad because you did not do all you could have done to prevent the death" or "you are bad because you were powerless to prevent the death."

As a result of this, your inner self feels alone.

You are attempting to deal with the terror of desertion by lashing out with anger.

This gives you the momentary feeling of "strength" that comes with anger, but it is a pseudostrength that is short-lived.

When you fill yourself with self-hatred, it spills over as anger toward others. You feel unworthy of receiving love.

Your hurt is compounded because you are chasing away the nurturing of people who care for you, which you need at this time more than ever.

Be careful not to berate yourself for feeling helpless and needy. It is far more heroic to have the courage to touch the depth of your suffering inner self than it is to act strong.

Forgive and nurture yourself through the pain. This will decrease your anger. Then you will be more open to receiving the care you need from others.

Your critical outer self has the positive intention of wanting you to be a more caring person. You can love it for its good intentions instead of responding with guilt to its heavy handed criticalness.

4

Pacts with God

"God, if you just give me another chance and bring them back, I promise I will never . . ."

Here the child part of you feels it is being punished for not being good enough and is bargaining with God as you may have done with your parents when you were a child.

Accept yourself with compassion. You will find God holding you in the quiet of your heart.

5

Deep Depression

The reality of the loss seeps in.

You feel hopeless because the greater part of you is still holding on emotionally to the memory of the person you have lost.

You may be telling yourself, "without him I can never feel happy or secure again."

At first, all you may be feeling is hopeless depression. This is a very painful way of holding on.

Your view of reality is skewed by your past habits and present pain.

You may have lost your favorite person in all the world.

Your commitment to them was so sincere that you would feel "unfaithful" to their memory to enjoy life without them.

You will soon see that the opposite is true.

The truth is that there are innumerable ways in which you can experience happiness and security and none of these require the presence of the one you love. Your new life can embody and represent a living endorsement of their preciousness.

6

CREATIVE
GRIEVING
PROCESS

This procedure has been helpful to thousands of people. By following it, you move yourself through the pain of loss and open the way to finding new strength in yourself. It has four stages:

1. Saying goodbye.
2. Nurturing your inner self.
3. Welcoming your true inheritance.
4. Feeling Gratitude

1

Saying Goodbye

If it is someone you love, imagine he or she is standing before you. Say goodbye to each of the attributes that was important to you.

Imagine a good friend, Margie, has passed away and you are speaking directly to her. Say: "Goodbye to your ability to love so openly and completely, to your quick wit, to your ability to remember a good joke, the closeness I felt from just being near you.

"Goodbye to your amazing ability to drive others crazy when you left things out of place, to your pig-headed resolve to be late to every movie opening, to your annoying habit of allowing the dog to sleep in the bed, to the way you looked when you were sad."

Think of each quality you will miss, negative and positive, knowing you will never experience her in quite the same way again.

"Goodbye to your long, soft hair, eyes that sparkle even when the sun didn't shine, weight you were always trying to lose."

Welcome the healing tears that well up as you slowly let go of each facet of that person who was so important to you.

You will never touch him/her again in this life.

2

Nurturing Your Inner Self

Remember having loving feelings for someone or something and breathe those into your heart. Let those loving feelings grow. Imagine holding your inner self in your lap as he or she cries and says goodbye to all of the specific qualities of the loved one you are missing. Fill the child with love and compassion as you exhale. *It will be very helpful to have someone you feel close to hold you physically as you go through this process.*

Usually an image of yourself as a child appears when dealing with grief. Breathe in and accept its pain. Fill the child with love and compassion as you exhale. Grief, like all other pain, comes and goes. If you lose someone very important in your life (a mother, father, grandparent, spouse, child), you may grieve many, many times over a period of years. Over time, it becomes less frequent, easier to accept, and of much shorter duration. Finally, the thought of the lost loved one may only provoke a momentary jolt of grief. A single tear, a bittersweet smile, and it is over. This is particularly true if you go on to step three. You are now ready to grow a positive bond with the spirit of your beloved that you never have to relinquish.

3

Your True Inheritance

This part of the process is the reverse of the first. Imagine that the person you lost is here right now.

Identify a specific quality about them that you miss most at this moment. It might be a number of things.

Choose that quality you most long for at this time.

Imagine seeing your lost one exhibiting that quality: strength, humor, vitality, understanding, affection.

Often it is a quality in yourself you would like to see flourish.

You might grieve different aspects of your loved one at different times.

Each time you miss the person, you have the opportunity of bringing back a valuable part of him or her.

Let's return to thoughts about Margie. At this moment the thing you miss the most about her is her warm, affectionate manner.

Spend several minutes simply watching your abdomen rise as you breathe in and fall as you breathe out. As you focus on your breathing your mind will become quieter.

Visualize your friend showing affection to you. Experience it in as many ways as possible.

Feel her soft touch of friendship on your shoulder.

Hear her merry laughter.

Bathe in the sunshine of her smile, the tilt of her head.

Notice how she listens intently to your latest adventure.

Recall her hug and encouragement.

Think of her affection as a form of energy that you can breathe in.

Let it come into every cell of your body, filling your heart and expanding the space around your heart.

Keep breathing it in until you are filled with her affection and love.

Now breathe that love out, beaming it to your grieving inner self.

Hold that part of you with all the energy your friend was able to muster.

This loving energy is a gift from her to your inner self. It is now yours to use.

Visualize yourself showing affection to someone else. See yourself giving a special look, a warm smile, a soft touch.

Accept your inheritance by writing it down or naming it, in this case, "affection."

Tape it someplace where you will see it often to remind yourself to use it.

Go into the world and practice using your inheritance.

Be affectionate to another person of your choice.

Each time you think of Margie, repeat the process and use her gift.

Do it at first, even if it seems awkward.

Soon, you will make the legacy of your friend's affection your own.

You will find it much easier to show authentic affection to yourself and to others than you could before.

Thank Margie often for your inheritance, by frequently showing affection to others.

If you have difficulty sensing the quality (in this instance, affection) practice the following exercise: Imagine walking over to the person in your mind.

Imagine that *you are* Margie.

Take on that persona physically and emotionally.

Imagine you are no longer imagining this.

You really are Margie.

Sense the wonderful innocence of affection growing within you with each breath.

Savor it.

Breathe it in through every pore of your body.

Then fill all the cells of your body with it.

Remember that this is a precious inheritance that comes from the one you lost.

You are in the process of making it a most valued part of your own personality, to be used again and again.

You can always remember Margie with joy and appreciation.

Sharing your newfound skill changes an inner feeling of scarcity and emptiness to one of generosity and fullness

In summary, when you remember the person you have lost and feel grief at the memory, find the quality you miss most about that person at this moment. Identify it. It may be the same quality you have practiced to develop before or a different one. Go through the process again, making it part of yourself.

The quality can even be one you disliked when he or she was with you. For example, it could be toughness, over organization, or poor driving skills. Extract and develop the aspect of that quality you can use and let the unwanted parts go. This technique is explained in more detail in the next chapter.

4

Feel Gratitude

Focusing on what you don't have is an act of rejection of yourself. It takes you out of loving flow. When you feel gratitude for your true inheritance, you are aligned with your higher self.

As you will discover in the next chapters, learning how to transform unacceptable parts of the person or thing you have lost into positive attributes will serve as a valuable learning experience that you can be grateful for.

CASE VIGNETTE OF
CREATIVE GRIEVING

*P*earl, a sixty-five-year-old practical nurse, came limp-
ing into the office. She looked very confused. She said
she repeatedly got lost when she went shopping and had
begun to spend most of her time at home. She had suffered
from this kind of memory loss for about six months. I asked
her if she had gone through some particularly difficult problem in the past six months. She told me that her nephew,
Billy, had been killed. She loved him very much. He would
come to her house every day, make sure she was safe and had
everything she needed. He shared stories of his girlfriends,
laughed at Pearl's jokes, and then, one day, he was killed in
an auto accident.

Pearl underwent such a tremendous shock that she
numbed herself to her loss. To stop the pain, she numbed
herself to everything around her. She could not go to Billy's
funeral, and failed to grieve for him, preferring to dismiss all
thoughts of him. As she numbed her grief, she also numbed
her awareness of the details of everyday life. Being unaware
of it, it was impossible for her to remember.

I showed her how to say goodbye to him. Pearl imagined
Billy on the other side of the room. She began to say goodbye

to his laugh, his hugs, the specific treats he brought her. Over and over again, she said "Goodbye, I love you Billy. I love how warm you were. Goodbye to your warmth."

When she stopped crying, I suggested that Billy's wonderful qualities were still available to her. The thing she missed most at this moment was his cheerful affection. She breathed it in and imagined filling herself with Billy's positive energy, taking him in through every pore of her body and filling each cell with cheerful affection. She was able to picture herself being filled by his twinkling warmth. Then she imagined giving that kind of affection to someone else. The circle was complete. By the end of the session, she no longer had to use confusion to ward off her pain.

On her next visit to the office, she greeted me with a cheery smile. Billy was obviously a part of her now. Pearl's memory was back to normal. She no longer lost her way when she left home.

7

TURNING A
NEGATIVE LEGACY
INTO A POSITIVE ONE

Often, the greatest grief occurs when you lose a person for whom you have ambivalent feelings. This is most pronounced with a deceased parent, but it can occur with anyone you have been in conflict with and longed to be closer to.

Suppose you had a mother who was physically or emotionally abusive much of the time. Despite this, you knew deep inside that she loved you. All your life you were torn between loving and hating her.

Follow these steps to find resolution of your conflict. Then you will be able to extract some positive attribute out of that person's behavior that will become a powerful asset to your personality.

1

Imagine your offending parent as a small child in a situation that molds him into his negative behavior pattern.

This chapter in part represents an adaptation of the work of Bob and Mary Goulding. See Goulding, R.L. and Goulding, M.M., *Changing Lives Through Redecision Therapy* (New York: Bruner/Mazel 1979).

2

Breathe in the discomfort or pain of that child who was to become your mother or father.

Touch his or her pain with your awareness and breathe out love and compassion.

Your breath holds your parent tenderly and lovingly as you exhale.

3

With this new understanding, forgive your parents for actions or words that harmed you.

4

Every harmful behavior or attitude demonstrated by your parent has buried within it some positive potential. For example, someone who is violent is attempting to be powerful. Extract a positive potential from your parent's undesirable behavior. Breathe that into every cell of your body.

5

Imagine yourself using that attribute in some current situation.

6

Practice using it over and over again until it becomes a habitual part of yourself.

My personal experience with my own father is a good example. Dad was very harsh and demanding of me when I was a child. He constantly criticized me for not being "tough" enough and for not being the best in whatever I tried. He was particularly abusive if he saw me sitting around, "doing nothing."

If I "talked back" to him, he would become furious. I became a shy child who was fearful of criticism from the outside world. I always felt inadequate—never good enough.

When my father died, I was grief stricken. Despite his abuse, I knew that he deeply cared about my welfare. He had been the motivating force in my life for many years.

I envisioned him as a twelve-year-old boy whose father had died. He was the oldest of seven children and was now the "man of the house." He spent much of his life driving himself relentlessly to take care of his family.

Knowing that, it was easy to feel compassion for him. I could understand that he drove me in the same way that he had driven himself. He wanted to insure my survival as he had insured his own.

Out of his dogged pushing and criticism, I extracted the attribute of strength and determination. Often, when I miss my father, I breathe in a spirit of strength and determination. I feel empowered. I have used this positive spirit of my father to carry me through many difficult situations.

A sense of inner strength and determination is now a comfortable part of myself that feels deep rooted. I use the sense of inner strength whenever I have to face a major problem.

I feel my father's presence supporting me in a wonderfully positive way that he was unable to do when he was alive.

Often, your negative emotional legacy when turned into a positive one is the very facet of your personality that you most need to enhance. There are two major reasons this occurs.

One is that you decide to be as unlike your parent as possible. The second is that you were intimidated from expressing yourself the way he or she did.

Both were true in my case. I did not want to be aggressively critical like my father had been. I was afraid of asserting myself with anyone because, as a child, I would risk Dad's rage whenever my opinion crossed his. I grew to expect that reaction from everyone.

Extracting the strength of assertiveness out of my father's abusive aggressiveness has been a wonderfully healing experience.

You can extract something positive out of any character trait, belief, or expectation your parents had that was detrimental to you.

INHERITED NEGATIVE RULES

Your legacy includes a list of "injunctions" or negative rules that were either consciously expressed or unconsciously mandated by your parents through their behavior. Some children follow these rules, some do not.

The influence of these injunctions plays a major role in the formation of your personality. Their effect in the course of your life continues unless you become aware of them and change them. They include:

"Don't be."

This is potentially malignant. A child is beaten physically or emotionally injured when he comes into his parent's presence. The unspoken and sometimes verbalized message is, "You have no right to live." Almost all suicidal patients have received this injunction.

"Don't be you."

This means, "Be how I expect you to be."

"Don't be a child."

Always be serious. You are supposed to be more like an adult. It is childlike to have fun.

"Don't grow."

Always stay a child so Mom and Dad can keep their importance as parents.

"Don't be successful."

This occurs when the parent is always critical and does not support successes.

"'Don't be close."

The parent avoids physical contact with the child.

"Don't belong."

Mom and Dad don't include the child in their closeness. Or they may be suspicious of outside groups.

"Don't want."

The child is shamed for wanting anything.

"Don't trust."

This occurs when the parents are unreliable and cannot be trusted or they are chronically suspicious of other people.

Stop for a minute and determine which injunctions apply to you. How are they currently affecting you life? *Reverse the message*. Your true inheritance turns them into positive affirmations. Write them down and practice using them every time you remember your parents.

POSITIVE DRIVERS

There are a number of "positive" drivers or admonitions you inherited that may have been well-meaning in intent but are subtly self-defeating. They include:

"Be perfect."

There is no such thing as perfection. If you try to be perfect, you will never enjoy the process of whatever you are doing because you fear that it will not live up to your expectations. No matter how good you do something, you always feel like a failure because you have not lived up to your own impossible expectations for yourself. Trying to be perfect is an invitation to failure. It produces a feeling of constant insecurity. You are never good enough. You also tend to attack the people you "love" for being imperfect. "If I am supposed to be perfect, anyone connected to me has to be perfect also. Their imperfections are a threat to my image."

"Be strong."

This one is usually addressed to men—sometimes to women also. It means that you are not supposed to have "weak" feelings. You must never be afraid. You should not be sad. You certainly must never cry. Love is mushy. You are applauded if you act like Rambo, battling your way through the world without feeling anything. You are unable to ask for or receive emotional support for yourself or give it to others. You become isolated emotionally from people who would like to be close to you and might scorn them for being weak. In the extreme, you only seek power and could become sadistic.

UNSPOKEN NEGATIVE DRIVERS

You may have received unspoken negative messages that become a self-defeating driving force in your personality.

"Don't be well."

The only time a child gets quality attention is when he is sick.

"Don't think."

The child is scolded for having its own opinions. A child should be seen and not heard. When he speaks, he should only echo the opinions of Mom and Dad.

"Don't feel."

This injunction is similar to "Be Strong," only a bit more inclusive. As a child, you are derided for showing emotions. Any emotion you feel is criticized as excessive or wrong: "You are not supposed to feel this way." Instead of reacting emotionally to things, you are supposed to be rational and think about them. Your intellect is applauded and your emotions are, for the most part, ignored.

"Don't do."

Mom and Dad take care of everything and are over-cautious. You feel anxious when you take any autonomous action.

"Please me."

If you act, think or feel in a way that is not pleasing to Mom and Dad, you are scolded or made to feel guilty because they act hurt. Your whole life is designed to please your parents. From this you decide that you must please everyone around. You are guilty if you do not. At the extreme, you spend your whole life doing this, and you lose touch with what you really want for yourself. What you lose, of equal importance, is the loss of your free choice to please others out of love—to decide freely to please someone just because it feels good to do it as a loving act.

"Try harder."

If you obey this driver, you can never do anything at an enjoyable, natural pace, because you will always have to try harder. As with the "Be Perfect" admonition, you can never try hard enough.

These messages become drivers for your whole life. Your outer self beats your inner self into living up to them. You learn to motivate yourself to do things through fear of disapproval if you do not follow the drivers.

You are afraid that if you do not live up to them, you will disappoint your parents, you will be criticized by them, rejected by them, or even abandoned. Living under the yoke of these drivers becomes your principal way of being in the world. It is always accompanied by physical tension. This is an underlying cause for stress and plays a major role in producing physical disease.

Pause for a few minutes and determine which of these drivers are affecting you at this moment.

Are you reading this book in a relaxed and enjoyable way that enables you to take it in and feel good about what you are learning? Are you "trying harder" to understand everything? Are one or more of the drivers pushing you? As we go on to further chapters, you will find it easier to follow through with the following alternatives. *These antidotes to the drivers are your true legacy!*

"Be perfect."

Instead of being perfect, enjoy your own abilities— whatever they are. Since your energy is not tied up in your fear of not doing something perfectly, you are able to focus better on what you are doing. Your performance improves, and your skill in doing it grows at a faster pace. Your motivation to do something well comes from your satisfaction and pleasure in doing it rather than from a fear of not being perfect. There are a vast number of circumstances that determine how competently you will be able to perform an activity on a given day: things like your past experience with it and your physical fatigue. You must also consider other important issues going on in your life that demand your energy and attention. All of these have to be taken into account and compassionately considered as you decide how much energy is reasonable to focus on the activity.

"Be strong."

It is human to have feelings. You are not a machine. Feelings are necessary in order for you to evaluate your life and to change it—to take care of yourself. "Being Strong" causes you to obscure your own needs and to be obtuse to the needs of others.

"Don't feel."

Dealing with things on a strictly intellectual level is boring. It makes it impossible for you to relate intimately with others and takes the passion out of life. To overcome a pattern of avoiding emotions, stop suffocating yourself. Practice by stopping whatever you are doing several times a day and identifying which emotion you are having, however minuscule in intensity it is. Are you joyful, anxious, sad, angry? If you feel bored or numb, ask yourself what emotion may be hidden inside, waiting to come out.

"Please me."

With the exception of an emergency, you should always consider yourself first. How are you feeling? What are your needs at this moment? And then when you make a decision to please someone else, do it freely and enjoy your contribution to them as a loving act. This does not imply that you are to become selfish. If you decide that your loved ones' needs are more intense than your own, enjoy the pleasure of generously giving and putting your own needs on the back burner for now.

"Try harder."

You will be much more effective and efficient if you

take into consideration your own natural physiological, emotional state as you engage in an activity. If you try hard to hit a home run, your body becomes tense, and you will probably miss the ball. If you relax and simply enjoy watching the ball come and swing the bat freely, you have a much better chance of succeeding.

8

GUILT

Perhaps you are beating yourself up for something you did or did not do in reference to the person who died. You may have spent years fighting with or neglecting the person you can no longer be with. "If only I had a chance to talk to him I could have explained it all. I may even have been able to prevent his dying."

Whether or not these recriminations are true, it is important not to worsen your guilt by attacking yourself.

CASE VIGNETTE OF GUILT

I know of a Vietnam veteran who fired his machine gun indiscriminately into a group of civilians in a fit of desperate rage when his buddy was killed by a sniper. For years he had nightmares about it. He felt tortuous guilt whenever he saw a child, because it reminded him of the children he killed. His guilt ended when he finally realized that every minute he spent feeling guilty about the dead children, he could spend helping the lives of the children who where still alive. He became a very active, effective leader in a worldwide campaign to feed hungry children.

What does your guilt have to teach you? How can you use that learning in your present relationships?

If you believe you really did hurt the person you are grieving, take some time and speak to them as if they were still here. Ask for their forgiveness. Tell them how you will be using their memory to benefit others now.

9

WHY IS IT SO
DIFFICULT
TO GRIEVE?

CRYING IS HEALING

When someone close to you dies, it touches off early childhood fears of abandonment. These and other painful echoes going back to infancy are touched off in your memory bank by your current loss. Therefore you experience not only your current agony but also earlier ones. Loss hurts. When you are deeply hurt, crying is a natural and healing response.

At the same time, you are reminded subconsciously and perhaps even consciously of early admonitions like, "Don't cry," "Don't be a baby," "You should be ashamed of yourself acting that way," "Control yourself." These admonitions are particularly caustic toward men: "Don't be a sissy," "Men don't cry."

It is appropriate to feel helpless for a while. When you experience severe pain, a large part of you is unable to focus on other things. You need support and love. All you are capable of doing is grieving. In addition, you are overcome by the overwhelming reality that you are helpless to prevent death. At these times you need all of the hugs and practical support you can get. You are dependent on others for this help.

It does not mean that you are falling apart if you express all of this with tears. Quite the contrary. It means that you are strong enough to express your authentic emotions. It takes courage to do so. To grieve is to admit that major change has occurred in your life. The unknown replaces familiar patterns and roles you have taken in your life. Your whole "reason" for living may have to be changed and expanded. It is tempting to avoid these issues by avoiding grief altogether.

10

AVOIDING GRIEF
AVOIDS LIVING

Facing the pain of grief opens you to new dimensions for living a deeper, richer life. Avoiding grief carries you off on a shallow path that can deaden you to deep emotions and even to life itself.

Our natural inclination is to avoid pain. Grief is the deepest of emotional pains. Many people avoid the emotion by holding their breath or breathing in a shallow fashion. They tighten the muscles that surround the area where the pain is located and focus their mind on something else.

Medical statistics show that the onset of cancer, heart disease, and other major illnesses often occurs within a year of a major loss in the life of a patient. Avoiding grief by going off on some addictive behavior trip leaves your body behind to grieve in the only way it knows how—through disease.

The substitute focus often has an addictive, compulsive quality to it. To stop it means you will feel pain. "Living" a life of addiction ultimately produces much more pain than grief does. Common addictions are alcohol, drugs, work, sex, gambling, and over-protective parenting. It can be anything that occupies much of your time and energy and keeps you from addressing your loss. Sometimes, the addiction takes the form of a chronic, automatic emotion—depression. Depression dulls your senses to everything. The usual purpose of the addictive behavior is to avoid pain and/or (as in the case of anger) to find some sense of inner "power." This power is sought to overcome the vulnerable sense of helplessness that is felt when confronting death.

CASE VIGNETTE OF
AVOIDING GRIEF

Nathan, a thirty-five-year-old lawyer, illustrates a particularly poignant example of being addicted to sex. Both of Nathan's parents died within a twelve-month period. His father had committed suicide. Nathan was coerced into coming to my office because his family was concerned about his offhand comments that he wished he were dead. He drove his car recklessly and drank heavily.

Nathan identified strongly with his father who was too "strong" to show "sissy" emotions. Nathan had a loving wife and son to whom he felt protective in a cold, distant way. He readily admitted that he was thinking of killing himself. After all, his father did it. Why couldn't he? Life *was meaningless to him. The only excitement he found was in finding new mistresses he could control sexually.*

Every time he was reminded about the loss of his parents, he would make some nonemotional comment like, "There is nothing I can do about it," and think of his mistress. He spent more and more time lavishing her with money. He expected loyalty and prolonged sex on demand whenever he wanted it. When one mistress tired of his control and left him, he would shrug it off and go out and "buy" another one. Nathan was unconsciously attempting to avoid his vulnerable feelings of abandonment by controlling women sexually.

During the three sessions he came in to see me, he did manage to feel enough affection for his wife and son to give some meaning to his life. He decided not to kill himself because it would cause them pain. His son needed a father. He didn't want anyone else to take over that role if he were out of the picture.

Relieved of the threat of suicide, Nathan quit therapy without learning how to grieve the death of his parents. Eighteen months later I learned that Nathan was diagnosed with cancer of the throat. Cancer in that region of the body is rare in nonsmokers, which Nathan was. It is not too far-fetched to consider that the cells in his throat had found their own way of "crying."

11

CAN YOU REALLY
LOSE SOMEONE
YOU LOVE?

The physical lives of Abraham Lincoln, Mahatma Gandhi, and Martin Luther King, Jr., were snuffed out by assassins who attempted to kill them. Their presence, however, is evident in one form or another inside the lives of millions of people. Their spirit continues to grow, and their effect on the world is far greater today than it was at the time of their physical death.

The same can be true of the person you have lost. I attended funerals for my mother and father many years ago. Their lives are a bigger, more positive part of me now than they were before the funerals. My love for them is no longer eroded by the negative parts of their personalities. Their desirable attributes continue to grow like a shining light deep inside of me. In many respects, they are much more alive in me now than they were when I could reach them on the telephone. I frequently reach them through the circuits of my heart and talk to them freely, and I don't get a bill for it at the end of the month.

I began feeling a little sad as I wrote this. It is a Wednesday evening and I would usually be out dancing at this time. I had promised to give someone a copy of this book in a few days and decided to stay alone in order to complete it. The sadness was centered within my chest. I closed my eyes and could see a sad little three-year-old "Arthur boy" huddled in his bed alone. Then I could see my mother bending down lovingly to hold him. There was a kind smile on her face.

I then tried to picture her with me now. I couldn't quite see her face, but her message was clear. She was encouraging me to go ahead with some plans for a romantic vacation I was thinking of taking in the near future. Mom was proud of my work, but romance was always the closest thing to her heart.

The "spirit" of my mother living in my memory was telling me to keep romance in my life. Now my higher self is chiming in with the wisdom that all of life can be a romance—even writing a book on grief. It is a pleasure to wonder about the next thought that might venture through my mind. How will my thoughts touch you, my reader? I feel more excited sitting here now contemplating the romance of writing than I would feel dancing. Thank you, Mom. You came through again!

Even as I write this, I am living testament as to how the creative grieving process can keep the spirit of your loved one very much alive.

12

CONFRONTING
YOUR OWN
MORTALITY

LOSE A BODY,
GAIN A UNIVERSE

Confronting death forces us to confront our own mortality. From the day we are born, cells within us get old and die. Our body serves as a wonderful vehicle that we use to learn, to work, and to procreate in. At each stage in life, it flowers in a manner that best suits our needs.

With age, the miracle of the body wrinkling and falling apart does a wonderful job of furnishing a home for the elder sage. It takes peacefulness, attentiveness and moving very slowly to appreciate the wonder of each moment and the spiritual splendor of the universe. As our body slows physically, our mind has the opportunity to grow spiritually. If we continue to use the aging process as a natural womb for spiritual growth, we are well prepared. At the end, our final breath signals wonderful relief from our worn-out outer shell and rebirth into pure spirit. Like a wave returning to its mother ocean, we return to our essence. In many cultures, this is a cause for celebration.

A winner is somebody who is excited by the opportunity of learning when he loses. We win in the dying process if we open up to it as a peaceful learning experience as we lose our life.

CELEBRATING THE JOURNEY

One of the greatest traditions in my home city, New Orleans, is the jazz funeral. (It is usually reserved for musicians, but I hereby serve notice that I request one for myself). Friends, relatives, and anyone else who wants to join in, follow a band playing sad music to the cemetery. Tears are shed for the physical loss. Coming back from the cemetery, the band explodes with joy, playing rousing versions of "When the Saints Come Marching In." Everyone dances and sings their way back to a celebratory feast. The loved one is sent off with a bang to the next stage of their journey.

DEATH AS AN ILLUMINATION OF LIFE

We question what really happens after death. Does our spirit or soul persist? Do we return to life in another form? Religion helps us to deal with these questions. One thing is certain (at least at the time this is being written) and that is that we all will die. We can spend our remaining days fearing this unknown ending to life as we know it or running away from it as if it will never happen. A far better approach is to use it as an illumination of our life.

Death may best be used as a searchlight that reveals the preciousness of each moment we have to live. Know that every moment of life is a wonderful gift to be savored with loving appreciation and excitement about the miracle of life.

Imagine now being on your deathbed looking back at your life. What would you have done differently? How does the way you are spending your life now meet those deathbed wishes?

Live your dream now before it is too late. Try doing the same for the person who has recently died. Imagine how he or she might have wanted to have done things differently.

You are the loving heir of your loved one's aliveness. Would it be meaningful to you to change your life in some way so that they can live their dream through you? You can find your own way of doing it so that it does not compromise what is important to you.

13

GRIEF
FREES YOU

You put a major portion of your life's energy into developing a persona or ego. You further molded your ego so that it meshed with the person you have lost.

You might think of that persona as a little piece of a jigsaw puzzle designed to mesh with another little piece close to you. Your fit with the neighbor piece gives you a sense of fitting in with the whole puzzle. When the death of a loved one occurs, the little piece you fit into so neatly is gone. The persona you molded especially for your loved one has no place to fit in. You custom designed it for that one special space. It can fit in nowhere else in the jigsaw puzzle. That piece is worthless. In fact, the whole puzzle is worthless without the missing piece. You might as well throw out the whole puzzle. Lost in the persona of that little piece, you feel worthless in a world that no longer fits for you. You feel as if you are nothing in a hostile world that has no secure place for you. You are a homeless waif.

That is how you may be feeling now. The reality of the situation is that you are the one who developed that little piece that has no place to go. In fact, you are the creator of the whole puzzle. The puzzle represents one picture of the universe as you have experienced it so far in your life. The out-of-place little piece you feel yourself to be represents a persona that you developed to fit in with the neighbor piece that disappeared.

Think of it again from the vantage point that you really are the one who creates both the little piece and the whole puzzle.

Putting it into religious terms, God gives you the material (all of the energy in the universe). Out of this you create your picture of the world (the big jigsaw puzzle) and your persona (ego)—the little piece that you design to fit in both with your outside world and the person you lost. The wonderful news is that you have the power to use this God-given energy (life) to produce any number of different personae and to change the whole puzzle.

Note again the chart on pages xvii and xviii, and see what a small space one's ego occupies, and the limiting characteristics it encompasses in Table B. You can create any number of personae. You can develop any personality trait you wish. As a human being in a society that is constantly changing at a faster and faster pace, it is necessary to stay flexible enough to do this.

Death wrenched you painfully out of a familiar place and way of being in the world when you lost your loved one. The skills you developed to fit yourself into that place are never lost. Those skills along with the skills that are your true inheritance from your beloved make it easier for you to create a new persona for yourself. It is never too late in life to do this. People who feel and act young at an advanced age do this all of the time.

In the remainder of this chapter, we will be looking at some particular life roles or personality traits that are disrupted by the loss of a loved one. Each one could represent a major part of your ego or self-image that you have emphasized or designed to fit in with your personal view of the outside world and your lost relationship.

As a prototype, let's begin by describing what occurs when your mother or father dies. We will start with the damage that occurs, and I will then describe how that particular persona may be recast.

RECASTING ROLES
IMPAIRED BY LOSS

The Role of Son or Daughter or Child

Your mother dies. No matter how old you are, a large part of your ego is vested into the role of a child who has an older person there to take care of him or her. That child part of you could only feel safe knowing that she was around. Giving up all the thoughts, feelings, and behavior you experienced in your role with your mother is painful. The child inside you is terrified of losing it all. Not only will you have no one there to take care of you, you will also have no one to relate to in the manner that you related to your mother. This fear is often greater if the relationship was a poor one.

CASE VIGNETTE

*A*nnette, *a forty-year-old woman whom I worked with, spent a large part of her life energy trying to please and live up to her critical mother's expectations. She never felt totally accepted. When her mother died, her grief was devastating. Now she would never have the opportunity to* *obtain that acceptance (love) she craved. Equally crippling was the void left by the absence of her mother's expectations. Her major motivating force in life—pleasing her mother— was gone. With "no reason to live," she became suicidal.*

By repeatedly doing the "Reversing the Negative Inheritance" procedure, Annette eventually was able to substitute a loving-inspired mother internally into her personality. Over a two- to three-month period, Annette began to truly love herself. By practicing the inner-self meditation many times a day instead of criticizing herself, she experienced heartfelt compassion and caring. She in effect installed a new inspiring mother into her psyche to replace the old well-meaning but critical mother who died. Instead of designing her life to please someone else, Annette was now free to create an autonomous life of her own.

RECASTING YOUR INJURED ROLE

There is learning and value to be obtained from any past experience. The experience you had living in the persona, playing the role you established before the death occurred, makes you an expert at using the particular personality traits developed for that persona. All of that persona wasn't created in vain. Understanding the value of those parts of your personality and using them in a manner that is beneficial for all parts of you creates a stronger you with deeper dimensions.

Annette, in her efforts to please her mother, had developed many positive qualities that were endearingly childlike. She radiated enthusiasm when someone cared for her or gave her a gift. She was very open to receiving physical caring. She laughed freely and had a childlike spontaneity that engaged people. This same spontaneity freed her to be creative about little things. When she gave up the self-criticism, she was able to use her creativity in her profession.

The persona of "child" will always be there as a valuable "self" for Annette to go into as her principal way of being in the world at appropriate times in the future, e.g., when she realistically needs to be taken care of by someone else, when she wants to play in an uninhibited manner, or in the early phases of creating something new.

These attributes can be valuable to her as personality traits that lighten more adultlike personae she develops.

It is very helpful to identify what role, life position, or principal character traits were prominent for you in relating to the deceased. Then you can begin to fill the void by finding healthy ways of employing these elsewhere.

Here are a few more examples:

The Role of Parent

There is probably no grief more painful than the one that occurs when you lose a son or daughter. If the child was very young, you had to pour all of your energy into becoming a good mother or father. The quality of loving care you developed is a valuable asset to maintain for anyone or anything you have contact with in the future. It is an essential component for fulfillment and deep engagement in life. The big difference is that you do not have the life and death responsibility you had that went with it when you nurtured a small child. It is very liberating to discover how to be caring and loving without feeling responsible for the welfare of others.

The Role of Lover

You lose your sweetheart. In some respects, this is similar to losing a child. The answer is the same. You have lost an object to love that gave you much pleasure, but all is not lost. The sweetness of your heart always remains a part of you. The skills you learned in developing one intimate relationship are a permanent part of yourself. They can be modified and used to develop new relationships. No, you are not being unfaithful to the memory of your lover. The specialness of that love need never be taken out of your memory bank.

The Role of an Aggressive Go-Getter Relating to a Passive Partner Who Dies

You no longer have an appreciative receiver or audience for your bold efforts. What is the point of being "strong" if there is not a more passive person to be strong for? Grief wrenches you out of this comfortably familiar pattern.

It provides a golden opportunity for evaluating the facet of you that is threatened by the loss and changing it if that seems desirable. Your legacy from the passive person who died might well be to learn how to enjoy the passive, receiving part of yourself and not have to maintain the burden of always being the assertive giver.

The Role of the Passive Partner Who Has
Lost an Assertive Mate

It is essential to be passive when you are tired or ill. Your persona is creating a healing nest for you. It is wonderful to be able to be the receiver when you want to be—but you haven't really lived until you've felt the joy of speaking out from your heart and walking your talk. Enjoy the feeling of autonomy it gives you to express your assertiveness.

If you are used to your partner taking over, it might be frightening for you to adopt the assertive role at first. But if you practice it each time you miss him or her, soon you will feel the thrill of enjoying your own competency and assertiveness.

When you succeed in doing this, grief turns into a goodbye to your own fixed way of being and an exciting hello to new ways.

You probably have witnessed a number of people who seem happier and more alive a year or so after their spouse has died. It does not mean that they had a poor marriage. It is an indication that they have grieved successfully and have used the experience to grow.

Instead of clinging to the past, which makes you a corpse in the present, creative grieving helps you to live fully in the present.

14

CREATING A
NEW LIFE
FROM YOUR SOUL

MOVING PAST
THE STUCK PLACE

A loss may cause depression by repeatedly drumming up images of yourself in your lost relationship. My favorite Zen saying is appropriate here: "He who is concerned with images is like a traveler loaded down with baggage. He can barely move. He who is free of images can move freely and travel anywhere."

If you do not accept the reality of impermanence, you are loaded down with pictures of the past, of the one who has left, and you stay bound to relating to the physical image of someone no longer there. You feel sad because there is no one there to join your own image. You keep struggling to reproduce your past history in order to stay the same. You may be so stuck in the image that you literally cannot move. You might want to stay in bed, living sadly with those old pictures.

By nurturing the pain as you experience it, you learn how to let go and give up those old images. You begin filling the void by actively using your psychological inheritance. You are not leaving your loved one. They are part of your new self. Your union can be even stronger, like two waves descending into the ocean. You are both part of the ocean. The spiritual components of your being join in a greater whole.

You can be with each other in the deep sea of your essence. Here is how you can become true soul mates, a procedure that will help you experience being a soul-mate with the person you have lost.

JOINING THE SOUL OF YOUR BELOVED

If you look at "The Real You" (on page xvii), you see the soul as the center of the bull's eye. When you quiet the dialogue between the inner and outer self, e.g. a typical dialogue at this time might be your outer self telling your inner self: "You are not strong enough, you cannot do this, you cannot do that." Your inner self replies, "You are right. I am helpless. I cannot live without him."

Being caught in this inner dialogue keeps you separate and alone. The following meditation on the breath of life quiets the dialogue and allows you to move automatically into your soul self.

Here you are in God's presence. There are no separate identities, no separation into physical bodies. You are in contact with your essence.

MEDITATION ON THE BREATH OF LIFE

1

Sit with an erect posture, but not stiffly.

Let your muscles nest comfortably into your spinal column. You are not leaning fearfully forward into the future nor clinging back to the past. You are upright, living fully in this present moment.

2

You may either close your eyes or leave them open, softly unfocused.

3

Take a deep breath, breathing deep down into your

abdomen so that it expands like a balloon as you inhale.

Let all of the air out, allowing your abdomen to flatten as you breathe out.

(Repeat this deep breathing three times).

4

Breathe naturally.

Your in-breath is like a gentle wave of loving energy carrying you down to a quiet place deep inside of you.

Your exhalation is another gentle wave driven by the wind of your out-breath, carrying away all thoughts and feelings in its path.

You can focus on your breath by feeling your abdomen rise and fall.

5

If your mind is racing, that is OK.

Simply become mindful of that and return gently to listening to your breathing.

If you find it difficult to focus on your breath, it will help you to count your breaths from one through ten.

Keep doing this until your mind quiets, then stop counting and simply attend to your breath.

Say to yourself "in" as you breathe in and "out" as you breathe out.

Now focus particularly on the quiet space between breaths. You are aware of the inhalation and exhalation, but your mind lingers more and more in that quiet space.

6

Keep this up for about twenty minutes.

With practice, you will reach a state in which your body (represented by your breathing), mind, and spirit are one.

Eventually you will be able to reach this state in a few minutes.

If you become anxious or restless, note that and continue the meditation.

The anxiety comes from the fear of letting go of your ego. Know that in a moment you will experience an exquisite sense of peacefulness. You are descending into the quiet place of your God in hiding.

Sense your whole being settle into the empty space

between breaths, the place that exists before the next thought arises.

Rejoice in discovering inner peace. Feel the God spirit holding your love. You are in your Buddha space. You are one with creative, universal energy—you are experiencing the true essence of yourself.

All that has ever been created dwells in this timeless, spaceless center of divine energy. Here, all things "inter-be." The quality of "thought" in this quiet place comes from your higher self. It is soft and mystical, like a gentle dream.

There are no sharp "have tos" or "try hards." No "expectation." Here you simply permit ideas, pictures, sounds, feelings, and words to arise as they will.

Because all things and people arise from this same ever-present source, it is a place of inter-being, of divine interconnectedness.

Open your heart to the spirit of your deceased. Feel their presence in you and your spirit in them. You are soul mates. Experience his or her most desirable qualities deep inside of you. Know that they are yours.

Each time you remember your "lost one," those new assets weave themselves deeper into the very fiber of your being. With the help of your higher self, as you nest in the soul part of yourself, permeated with the loving energy of the creator, you can become a cocreator of a transformed, new you.

The death you faced left a space in your life that you can now embrace as an opening. It frees you to break out of old patterns and to discover new, more satisfying ways of being. Using your new assets, you can move through that space as a brave explorer in the virgin territory of your existence.

You can use this same meditation any time you are confused or at a new life crossroad or to seek deeper understanding. For instance, you might be wondering, "What's the use? Why was this person in my life? What is the higher (divine) intention of it all?"

Pose the question with your conscious mind, repeat it mindfully five times, then let it drop out of your conscious mind. Proceed with the meditation on your breath and let your mind become quiet. The answer will come to you in the form of whisperlike words or a daydream.

You may then see yourself as an active messenger for the departed. You do this by seizing the moment and emerging heroically into the future using your loved one's attributes in your own special way.

When I focused a few moments ago on the higher meaning of my life with my father, I found my enthusiasm and determination to complete this book reach an exhilarated high. The writing flowed easier. It is as if his aggressive, determined spirit were writing the book with me.

When the grief has become a minor part of you, you can continue to benefit greatly from the meditation whenever you are tense, unhappy, or undecided. You may not even think of the departed at these times. He or she is truly a part of you.

With the old patterns of life disrupted and new ones in the process of forming, it is time to bring new vision into your life.

YOUR HIGHER SELF
CAN ADVISE YOU

You can use the procedure described previously or the following modification of it to receive answers from your higher self that will give you a start in a direction best fit for you at this time.

1

Take a deep breath and hold it.

As you hold your breath, ask yourself one question. Some questions you might ask are:

What aspect of my life should I focus on now?

How should I change my job or profession?

How can I use my spiritual self in everyday life?

How can I have more fun in life?

What changes would be most beneficial to make with my friends and family?

If you cannot think of a concrete question to ask yourself, ask the question, "What should I be questioning in my life at this time?"

Then proceed with the meditation using the question that comes up as a response.

2

Take a deep breath in and hold it for a moment. Let your breath out and allow the question to flow out of your mind.

3

Focus on your breathing as described on page 107.

As your conscious mind quiets, you are opening the doorway to your higher self.

4

Out of the quiet, a gentle thought or image like a daydream will emerge.

This contains the answer you are seeking.

If the response is unclear, repeat the procedure.

5

Write it down and find some practical ways to bring your vision into your everyday life.

15

GRIEF AS A RESULT
OF DIVORCE
OR SEPARATION

In any listing of major life stressors, divorce is listed at or near the top. Separating from any long-term loving relationship can produce lasting scars that erode your capacity for future intimacy if you fail to nurture yourself. It is true that divorce can be the best solution to a destructive relationship. But because of the havoc divorce produces, it is urgent to try to turn the marriage into a positive direction first. Often the destructiveness can be reversed with the help of expert counseling. If you still decide that you would be better off not married to each other, you can remain caring friends. This is essential if children are involved.

Space limits us here to ameliorating the sadness and grief that occurs after the decision has been made. For the rest of the chapter, the term divorce will be used in the generic context of the dissolution of any long-term relationship.

DIVORCE SHOCK

A feeling of shock, a sense that life has no purpose, emotional paralysis with a fear that any action carries with it the risk of another failure—these are common reactions to divorce. The shock that occurs is numbing, similar to a loss through death. The risk of losing yourself in a chronic depression is great unless you can let go by grieving.

THE TORMENT OF AMBIVALENCE

You cannot begin the grieving process until you accept the fact that the separation is real and assume that it is final. Then creative grieving can help you get on with your life.

There are some important issues that touch the very core of your personality and that need to be taken care of before you are able to fully let go of your partner.

A lovely, sensitive woman described her separation from her husband as torment because "The tree of love is dead, but our roots are intertwined. I can't let go." From this perspective, divorce or separation from a long-time lover or friend can produce chronic pain that is even more excruciating than the lancing agony of death. Many people linger in attached misery long after they have ample reason to separate. Others stay depressed for years after legal divorce has taken place. Depression here is an emotional way of hanging on. Its message is "I'll stay depressed until we get it right or until I'm loved again." Delaying the final split is due in large part to the fear of the hurt that will occur when you begin untangling the roots that still hold you together. Nurturing your inner self and using the creative grieving procedure will help you out of this no man's land.

It is painful to have to tear apart what brought you together initially and difficult to break up the cement that kept you together for so long. All of the facets of your personality are involved. The one you were close to was, at different times, a mother or father who took care of you, a companion to play with or to solve problems with, a child to love or to take care of.

Various facets of your personality that were undeveloped were bolstered by compensatory attributes in your spouse. For example, where you were shy, he or she may have been bold, and vice versa.

These dynamics are the same as those discussed in Chapter 13 of this book. Review that chapter. List the various roles you were in with your spouse and note which character traits you will miss. You can take care of them by using the same creative grieving procedures that are used when a loved one dies.

You may go through the same stages that a mourner of a death goes through: numbness, denial, anger and guilt, pacts with God, and deep depression (see Chapter 5).

There are many cultural biases and myths concerning divorce that influence you. These create hurdles that have to be overcome.

DIVORCE MYTHS

The more specific you can be in evaluating these myths for yourself, the more effective you can be in nurturing your inner self through the pain and in using creative grieving to strengthen yourself.

Despite the prevalence of divorce today, it still carries with it clouds of centuries of disapproval. These echo in your mind as broad blanket self-condemnations that anchor you to misery. Some of them may contain an element of truth. Facing the truth with compassion and self-forgiveness can help you to modify your behavior and grow to be more the caring person you strive to be. Let's verbalize a few of these self-condemnations in the exaggerated form they might take in your mind and consider a rational response:

I am socially unacceptable.

"I've committed the sin of breaking a sacred vow. I'm a threat to the community. I'll be a social outcast." Is it really a sin to give up unreconcilable differences and endless battles? Are you a bad person because you made a mistake in choosing a mate? Can you see the virtue in yourself for having the courage to learn from your mistakes and take action, to give up the destructive fighting and create a new life?

Your divorce does put a threat of instability into the world of those who were close to you as a couple. You can counter this by using your experience to verbally support the strengths in your friends' marriages instead of flaunting your freedom. You can maintain closeness with your true friends who are married and make a host of new friends with single people who understand what you are going through.

I am a terrible parent.

Your tender inner self remembers the terror of losing

your parents when you were a child. You assume that this is true of your children and add that onto any fears that they really do have. Your guilt can be so overbearing about this that you feel too paralyzed to go through with a separation that is in the loving best interest of your children.

One fourteen-year-old told me that when her parents separated when she was five, her predominant emotion was excitement about moving into a new place. She felt secure that both parents loved her and would never leave her. This is unusual. Most children do feel threatened. To minimize that, it is imperative that:

1. they be kept carefully advised about any major decision
2. visitations be spelled out and honored. A reliable schedule to see both parents in turn is reassuring
3. parents agree on restrictions and rewards
4. children should never be used as pawns in arguments or as a sounding board for criticizing your ex-spouse
5. children should be assured that they are not responsible for the break-up of your marriage

DAMAGED SELF-IMAGE

A break-up of any long-term relationship leaves you with a damaged image of yourself. These are some common causes:

Despite the reality that a large percentage of the population is unmarried, you are supposed to be part of a pair. If you are seen to be alone, it means there is something defective about you. You may actually believe that about yourself and imagine that others are thinking the same about you. For some, that feeling is so strong that it is tantamount to wearing a huge yellow patch saying: "Single . . . beware, I might be contagious. I failed the course on Relationships 101." You might add to this self-misery by becoming a fortuneteller and telling yourself: "I'll always be alone!"

There has been a major shift in the past ten years toward acknowledging and honoring the single life. Many professional women are choosing a career over marriage. Singles clubs and church groups provide social contacts and often act as an extended family. Your past experience with a relationship equips you better to enter a new one should you choose to do so.

GUILT ABOUT LEAVING

If you are the person who left, you are probably burdened with guilt. No matter how justified your reasons were for leaving, or how caring you are about the person you once loved and may still love, he or she is going to feel intense pain because of what you are doing. Even if you are certain that you are a good person, doing something that results in pain to someone else will never enhance your self-image as a Good guy.

As a caring person, feeling guilty is appropriate. Don't use it to punish yourself into depression. Don't try to ward off the pain of guilt by attacking your ex-partner. Do have compassion for yourself and the one you are leaving.

Be as generous as possible with your time, expertise, and money to help him or her create a new life without you. Ex-spouses can become wonderful lifelong friends.

At the other extreme, don't fall into the codependency stance: He or she can't survive without me. This is a discount of their potential. It builds up your ego at someone else's expense. It may cover over your fear that you can't live without that partner.

"Don't leave. I can't live without you!"

If you are the one left behind, your initial reaction is likely to be of shocked betrayal. "I organized my whole world around you and I trusted you with my very life, but you abandoned me. I must mean nothing to you. Without you, my life means nothing to me." These thoughts and reactions are magnified greatly if your spouse has been secretive about his or her intention to leave or has had an affair. You then might begin to hate your spouse for making a fool out of you. You may obsess about the other man or woman and direct your anger toward him or her. If you have low self-esteem to begin with, you may find reasons to attack yourself for not being what you imagine the other party to be. The important thing here is not to abandon yourself. You are never a fool for loving someone. Being able to love well is a powerful and positive attribute that you own, and that can never be taken away. Your ability to lead a full and happy life never has depended upon another person. Your spouse's presence may have made it easier to express particular parts of yourself because some aspect of his or her personality invited it, but what you expressed was yours and still is.

The list of self-criticisms and recriminations is end-less because the separation reactivates every feeling of failure and self-doubt you have had about yourself since childhood. Instead of ruminating about that, make your own list of things you might have done differently and write them down. Notice that there may be an element of reality about things you would like to change about yourself. What is the learning to be had? What part of yourself needs developing? You can turn your self-doubt into excitement about changing.

Divorcing someone frees you to marry new parts of yourself.

Exaggerated Negative Fortunetelling

Stories that you design to frighten yourself may be clog-ging your mind and keeping you inactive. A favorite one at this time is "I'll always be alone!" Realize that you are the author of the story. Turn the negative fortunetelling into positive visions directing your life forward.

You may be silently screaming to yourself: "I can't live without you." For some people, that voice is so strong that they commit suicide or threaten suicide in an effort to blackmail their spouse to stay. Others become so angry that they murder their spouse. "You have destroyed my life. It is only just that I take yours."

Can't is a word children use when they are afraid to be openly rebellious. Instead of saying "I won't," they play it safe by saying "I can't." In this situation, your inner child is saying "I won't go through the pain of saying goodbye." In the pressure of the moment, all parts of your ego may be overwhelmed by the loss, and you may actually believe "I can't survive."

Your husband or wife may have done a lot of things for you that you never learned how to do for yourself— balance the checkbook, budget, cook a meal, earn a living, use the washing machine, get the car serviced, be socially outgoing, express excitement. If you are like most people, you chose a mate that would make up for some real or imagined deficit in yourself. When confronted with losing all that, you may feel overwhelmed and truly believe that you can't survive.

If you look more closely at what you can do, you will discover that the mountain of impossible tasks facing you is just a series of simple or more complex molehills to get over.

Approached as a positive challenge, each one provides

you with an opportunity for growth. Wrestling with each one in turn is your personal, tailor-made prescription for growing self-confidence. You are correcting undeveloped parts of yourself that predisposed you to be overdependent on others. This will require effort, study, and sometimes professional help to achieve. The payoff is well worth the effort.

Meditating on the inner self and using the creative grieving process is a lifesaver here. Instead of buying "I can't," using these techniques will enable you to say "I will learn how to live without you and be a more complete person because of it."

The first "I can't" to deal with is, "I can't love myself. I need you to love me." Repeating the inner self meditation, every time you have an unwanted emotion, teaches you how to love yourself in a way that is all-encompassing. By using the creative grieving procedure, you identify what aspect of your ex-spouse you are missing. By being explicit and practicing the skill formerly missing in yourself that your spouse took care of, you are turning the helplessness of "I can't" into the powerful excitement of, "I am learning."

HEALING THE WOUNDS

Here is a summary of the steps you can follow:

1

Be very understanding of yourself. As each fear arises, smile at the exaggerations and support yourself through the real ones. You can take pride in the adventure of learning new things and creating a new life.

2

If you have feelings of depression or anxiety, or are angry much of the time, your outer self is not supporting your inner self. Carefully monitor and change self-criticism. At this most difficult time, your inner self needs all the love it can get, not castigation.

3

Replace criticism with the total self-love, compassion,

and acceptance that result from doing the inner self meditation outlined on page 28. Repeat the meditation each time you have an unwanted emotion. If there is something you did that truly warrants feeling guilty about, forgive yourself and use the guilt as an indicator that there is an important lesson to be learned. Forgive yourself and make a decision not to repeat that behavior in the future.

4

Monitor your behavior. If you are lost in compulsive activity (work, play, eating, sex, gambling, alcohol, drugs . . .), anything that you feel driven to do, you are probably avoiding the pain of grief. With compassion for your inner self, stop the behavior and start the creative grieving process.

5

Repeat the creative grieving process each time you miss your spouse.

SPECIAL ASPECTS OF
CREATIVE GRIEVING
IN DIVORCE

Grieving Personality Parts

All of the personality voids discussed earlier concerning losses through death may apply strongly to losses of long-term relationships. For example: If you are a creative romantic person who is separating from a practical planner, you will feel the fear of not having anyone around to plan things in a realistic manner. Your partner, on the other hand may feel dead without your creative spark around him or her.

Carefully following the creative grieving process enables you to build those missing characteristics into your own personality.

Grieving the Loss of an Intact Family

The picture of a loving mother and father with two or three happy children is a deep-seated dream. It provides an ultimate sense of security. It fills an inner void that has been present since childhood if that image wasn't a reality for you when you were a child. The thought of giving up the marriage brings with it the death of your dream. When you go through a divorce you reactivate all your childhood longing, compounding the grief of not having that sense of security in your life in the present, and possibly not in the future.

Whether you had family security or not, it is important to feel the pain of the loss and grieve it. Say goodbye to that essence of family love *as you pictured it*. When the pain has subsided, breathe in that essence: father love, mother love, child love, the strength of family togetherness. Give these wonderful qualities to your inner self and then practice giving it to your children. Repeat this process whenever you find yourself longing for an intact family. You are turning a dream into the real thing.

You might also be saying goodbye to special family activities—sitting around the dinner table, enjoying talking to each other. Let the feeling of pain go through you about the absent one and reproduce the activity with those who are there. Don't hesitate to add friends to the picture.

Free of the old conflicts, you can build a much stronger family unit than you had before.

OTHER LOSSES

There are often other people you have been close to that may drop out of your life with your partner. In-laws you were close to, mutual friends. If you move in addition, you lose your familiar surroundings, casual acquaintances, familiar places to shop, perhaps even your job. Both parties suffer a big financial loss. You may give up a pet or keepsake that had meaning to you. All of these were sources of security. Their absence intensifies your inner void. Do not discount their importance, but also don't make an inventory of loss and use it to overwhelm yourself. When you become aware of any one of them, say goodbye to it and replace it emotionally as described in Chapters 6 and 7. As soon as possible start finding things in your new environment to enjoy. Actively cultivating new friendships with people who have interests similar to your own will offset loneliness and build your self-confidence. Use the inner self meditation to take care of your sadness when it arises—not your new friends. They can share and support you in your excitement about your new life, but it is unwise to lean upon them to help you in your mourning about the past.

CASE VIGNETTE

Julie, a competent physician and loving tender mother left her husband who was emotionally unavailable and who physically disappeared whenever a crisis came up in the family. Julie had two small children. She felt relieved to be free of the constant disappointment and anger she felt about her husband's unavailability. She did very well with the divorce until she took the children to Disney-World. Confronted with hyperstimulated children that had to be kept within safe boundaries and being surrounded by intact families who were there with a mother and father, she found herself crying for the lost image.

After going through the creative grieving process, she realized that she had both mothering and fathering skills that were excellent. It would be wonderful to have a supportive spouse, but she was doing very well by herself. Her children were living proofs of this. They were much happier and more productive in school since she left her husband.

I am not advocating divorce here. I believe every available treatment modality should be tried in order to make the marriage viable, particularly if children are involved. Our goal here is to minimize the injury that accompanies divorce for all parties involved.

CASE VIGNETTE

Tony, a twenty-eight-year-old truck driver, was the father of three children. He was severely depressed following his wife's decision to stay separated from him. Tony spent his time thinking about her. He called her frequently, much to her annoyance. Finally, he decided he had to say goodbye. I explained the necessity of grieving—a painful and unavoidable experience, assuring him that eventually it would pass. I contrasted this with depression, which he produced in himself by constantly longing for his wife and feeling sad about her absence.

I asked him to picture his wife standing in front of him and to say goodbye to those qualities about her that he missed the most. For the next twenty minutes, he let himself feel the pain of his grief. He said goodbye to her smile, the feeling of love he had when he was out with her, the bond of family togetherness and the sense of importance he felt when she paid attention and expressed love toward him.

Then I asked him to imagine breathing in the quality that he most needed at this time. He imagined his wife sharing love and breathed the spirit of love into his body. He was able to feel it as a part of himself. He then visualized himself expressing love to his family and friends. Tony followed the same process each time he felt the pain of his wife's absence. His depression lifted within a week. He began to put his energy into finding a more satisfying job, going back to school, and renewing old relationships. As Tony's capacity to love improved, he established deeper, more positive relationships with his children. Six months later Tony's wife changed her mind and stopped the divorce process. The new Tony was the person she had always longed for.

16

GRIEVING
OTHER LOSSES

GRIEF OF TEMPORARY SEPARATION

You take someone to the airport and you feel like crying when the plane with your loved one leaves. You cannot bear to say goodbye. As you drive home, you smile and think of the person who has gone. The next time this happens, take the smile one step further. Breathe in the quality about them you are missing most at this moment. Fill yourself with that quality and, at the first opportunity you have, use your new quality with someone else or in some activity. You can do the same thing in the event of a minor separation. You feel abandoned and sad when your mate goes off to work. You feel a loss when your child leaves for school. The sadness can be used as a signal alerting you to how you are using the person who has left to fill in for part of your own personality that you might enjoy developing.

Practice using the quality about your loved one that you miss the most during the day. Make it a strong part of yourself. You will have more to share when the person returns later that day. Instead of clinging to the loved one you missed, you will be better able to enjoy them as an equal.

GRIEF FROM LOSS OF
A FAMILIAR PLACE

Vacation Sites

If you were traveling through a foreign country, would it dismay you to hear somebody say, "Oh, there's a McDonald's"? Even if you particularly like fast food restaurants, you would certainly want to see something different on your trip. However, there is always a part of you that wants to bring the familiar with you. You can do that. For example, I recall walking along a beautiful country road in France with a friend. There was a lovely old chateau in the distance. Rolling hills were dotted with vineyards on my right. On the left, cows chewed contentedly, looking up to see who we were. I spent fifteen minutes telling my friend about life in New Orleans, complete with its festivals and dancing, a place with perpetual movement—always something to do, someplace to go, someone to see. When I came home and walked the streets of New Orleans, what did I talk about? That's right. The wonderful tranquility of the French countryside! Your needs and mine change from moment to moment.

It is important for you to pay attention to your thoughts—what you require, and what you long for.

You may be surprised to learn that you do not have to go away on vacation or put your life on hold until you get to some beautiful place. You can bring the spirit of the place to you. The more you feel you need it, the more important it is for you to frequently bring that spirit to you. For example, if I feel agitated by all the noise and activity in New Orleans, I can pause for a moment and bring in the essence of a cow grazing peacefully, swatting flies with her tail while chewing. I bring that essence of France into me. I hear the birds singing, feel the sun on my skin, and the cool breezes. It is all part of me. I am the peacefulness of the French countryside.

You have the same recourse. The harder you work, the more minivacations of the mind you need.

GRIEF FROM LOSING YOUR JOB, MONEY, OR SOCIAL STATUS

Lose Money, Find Yourself

I tell you now a cautionary tale. I recently decided it was time to put money aside for retirement. Due to my habit of taking off to world destinations for training or vacations, my bank account was sparse. I estimated I could retire for about six months. I had a nice house, a good car. People I spoke to were of the unanimous conviction that I could make lots of money in real estate. Therefore, I took every cent I could borrow and invested it to the teeth. For a while, I took great pride in the adage, "You are what you own." I would see my holdings and say, "Hey, this is mine." I felt proud. A year later, the real estate market fell precipitously. I had to declare bankruptcy. Add to this a giant tax bill and you can see why I felt really poor. How do I feel about all this? Let's take a ride through my emotions. Fortunately, I still had my profession and could support myself and my family. I felt guilty and humiliated that I had to give up the house. Retirement? That was now the impossible dream.

For the first weeks, I was miserable. I grieved. I did, however, remember to support my inner self. Because of this, I stopped being self-critical. Instead of calling myself a failure, I told my tender inner self that he was much more than what he owned. I told him that I loved him whether he was rich or poor. I helped him say good-bye to all the material things he had enjoyed. It was painful to give them up, but when I looked closely at what I was giving up, I realized that those things did not constitute my security at all.

True security came from my ability to love myself, to give love, and to accept it from people who are important to me. It also came, in equal measure, from my ability to create.

When I realized this, I felt a sense of freedom and gratitude. I made a decision to never think of investing in anything but my own profession, i.e., in myself. I began to feel excited. I knew then, for the first time, that my self-worth had nothing to do with the amount of money I had in the bank, or the amount of things I was able to buy with that money. I had verbalized these adages before, but now I knew it to be true deep inside.

If you lose a job, your money, or some other material thing, if you lose social status, it's all the same. You can handle it with creative grieving.

1

Visualize your grieving inner self. Nurture him with your affection.

Above all, do not be critical of him. He is hurt enough by his losses.

Accept his grief by breathing it in.

Fill him with love and compassion as you breathe out.

2

Say goodbye to the different qualities of whatever you have lost.

For example, when I pass the beautiful home I had to give up, the quality I notice most about it was the noble English Tudor styling. I said goodbye to its nobility.

Say goodbye to those qualities that the material loss represents to you.

3

Breathe those qualities into your body.

As I walk past the house, I breathe in the sense of nobility. My posture straightens. My stride lengthens, I can feel myself being quite noble.

4

Ask yourself, "Are those qualities really important to me? Would it be meaningful to have them be a part of my personality?"

If the answer is yes, write them down.

Develop a plan for remembering to practice those qualities in yourself.

Visualize expressing them to someone, and then go out and do it as many times as possible every day until it becomes a part of you.

If you feel uncomfortable or anxious doing the new behavior, keep practicing it until it becomes automatic. If you do it for six weeks, it will become a wonderful new part of you. (I decided feeling noble was not quite what I wanted. I chose to feel "solid" instead).

MONEY GRIEFS

Are you one of the vast majority who never seem to have enough money? I remember vividly the fear I felt when I first lost all of my money. I briefly described how I handled the experience. Remember, the first step is to grieve its absence. This is not as simple as it sounds. What are you really grieving? For most people, it is a sense of security. For others, it is a loss of power. Still others spend many years working seventy hours a week so they will be "free" some time in the future.

I have the good fortune to be close to people from all walks of life. No two people who walk into my office are alike when it comes to money. I think of one elderly woman on welfare who said, "I've never had it and I've never missed it. I always knew, if I did my bit, the Lord would provide." On the other hand, I remember a millionaire many times over who kept himself anxious that he would not have enough money if his children or their children came down with some dreaded disease.

If you do need money, do not focus on money. Focus on what you can do in your life that will give you the zest that you imagine money would provide for you.

Then find a way to bring that zest into your work life. The money will come. It will create itself.

GRIEF OF MOVING TO A FOREIGN COUNTRY

The country you were raised in will forever be home to a part of you, no matter how well you adjust to new surroundings. A word, a song, a fragrance, a food flavor, or a familiar face that looks more like your own face will tug on your heart strings as you sadly recall what you left behind.

As with other griefs, it is important to grieve and say goodbye every time you miss something about your birthplace. When the move is fresh, you have much to grieve: family, relatives, friends, language, customs, climate, music, arts, dances, food. You may be overwhelmed with fear of the strangeness surrounding you, because many people feel insecure about foreigners. You may even be greeted with prejudice and rejection by your new neighbors.

To weather the stormy landing, you must have deep love and compassion for yourself.

1

Do the inner self meditation.

2

Say goodbye by letting yourself feel the pain of separation from whatever it was you held dear, that you are now missing.

3

Breathe in the essence of what you are missing. Feel it as part of yourself. Enjoy expressing it and using it whenever that is feasible.

Cook that special dish you are missing.

Read a story or sing a song in your native language.

Reach out and talk to someone from the old country.

CHERISHING YOUR ROOTS

I am not suggesting that you cling to the past. I am strongly advising that you cherish your roots and use them as a foundation for the present and future. When transplanting a tree, you have to be extremely careful to protect the root ball, to give it fertile soil, and then shower it with tender loving care. The same treatment should apply to you.

Don't deny your root heritage in an effort to become a part of your new country, because by doing so, you are being prejudiced against a valuable part of yourself. How can you grow and bloom in your new space if you are poisoning yourself with self-rejection at the same time?

EMBRACING YOUR NEW COUNTRY

Feeling solid with the values, customs, and rituals of your old culture, you can now meaningfully touch and become a part of your new community.

Use the strength you garnish from the past to give yourself the power to overcome the difficulties of becoming fluent in a new language.

Get to know as many new people as possible. Look for a church or support group you can be comfortable with. You don't have to give up your own religion to benefit from the spiritual communion of one that is foreign to you.

Be active in school and civic activities.

In each sector of the new country you venture into, in your work, religion, or play, you will find a wonderful opportunity to grow as you add exciting new twists to your own knowledge.

Be patient with things you don't agree with when they clash with your customs. If you turn your disdain into compassion, you can become a powerful force in making your community a better place to live in.

You have much to contribute to it and it has much to give to you.

SUMMARY

The more you practice taking care of your inner self in times of grief, the more you will be able to tolerate loss. You will increase your ability to face the reality of impermanence. The fear of loss is a major impediment to allowing your loving feelings to flow freely. From the initial fear of rejection to the ultimate loss through sickness and death, the fear of your own grief can make it too risky to really love someone. Practicing the creative grieving techniques helps you to engage in life more fully. It converts the grief experience into an opportunity for growth.

CONCLUSION

We peer into a microscope and see matter miraculously appear out of pure essence. Out of this same essence, we can create a new life for ourselves that emerges purified by the painful fire of grief.

Death illuminates what is important in life, and opens the door for new life. It is comforting and exciting to see death as just another phase of life.

As we see our beloved off on their new journey or experience the loss of something precious to us, it is wonderful to know that all people and things are interconnected. A part of them will always be with us on our new trip.

ABOUT THE AUTHOR

ARTHUR SAMUELS is presently an associate professor of clinical psychiatry at Louisiana State University Medical School and founder and director of the Stress Treatment Center of New Orleans. He is author of numerous published professional articles on psychotherapy, group therapy, the relationship between stress and physical illnesses, and stress prevention, as well as two previous books, *The Glory of the Inner Child* (published in German) and *The Three-Minute Therapist*.

Forty years of private clinical practice and teaching psychotherapy have given him clinical expertise. Going through the difficulties of his own life has given him compassion with others. He has learned to live more and more in the moment and to be comfortable with the fact that all knowledge is incomplete. He has learned to watch mindfully as fresh learning unfolds. This keeps him forever in a happy kindergarten of discovery instead of lost in the dust bins of old knowledge.

One of the most important things he has learned is to accept the reality that everything is impermanent. This gives him great freedom to enjoy the present moment fully. There is comfort in knowing that the spiritual essence of our loss remains with us as a valuable part of ourselves. We can use these parts as a celebration of our eternal tie with the departed and move on into a new phase of life. With this in mind, Dr. Arthur Samuels wrote *The Art of Saying Goodbye*.

TEACHINGS ON LOVE

Thich Nhat Hanh

*"We all need love. Love brings us joy and well-being.
It is as natural as the air."*

In *Teachings on Love*, world-renowned Buddhist teacher
and writer Thich Nhat Hanh shows how we can put
unconditional love into practice. Using anecdotes,
personal experience and a deep understanding of the
Buddha's way of mindful living, Thich Nhat Hanh provides guidance and inspiration to help us foster and
deepen all our relationships.

He offers us teachings on self-love, nourishing
happiness, deep listening and loving speech, living
mindfully together and methods of resolving conflicts,
together with meditations on love and ways to heal
relationships with our families.

Thich Nhat Hanh is the widest-selling Buddhist
author in English worldwide. He lives in a meditation
community in France, and travels the world teaching
"the art of mindful living".

ISBN 0 00 714761 9

365 DALAI LAMA

DAILY ADVICE FROM THE HEART

His Holiness The Dalai Lama

Imagine having an audience with the Dalai Lama where he could offer you personal advice on how you could live your life better, be more joyful and create a better world. This amazing book brings you exactly that: short passages to offer you enlightening advice, day by day, including meditations on:

* the stages of life: for the young, adults and the elderly
* life situations: for men and women, single people, families, the wealthy, the poor, the sick, the dying and those who care for them, and others from all walks of life.
* your state of mind: for the happy, the sad, pessimists, optimists, the suffering, the isolated, the angry, the proud, the abused, the shy, the undecided, those with no self-esteem, the indifferent
* society and the world: war, politics, education, farming, the environment, business, and the future
* your spiritual life: for believers, those who have no religion, contemplatives, those who have great faith, those who want to become Buddhists, practising Buddhists.

ISBN 0 00 714797 X

EMPOWERING YOUR SOUL THROUGH MEDITATION

Rajinder Singh

Empowering Your Soul Through Meditation explores the power and energy of the soul that is within everyone and how we can use it to transform our lives. Rajinder Singh awakens us to the "empowered soul" and its rich qualities such as unlimited wisdom, fearlessness, immortality, unconditional love, connectedness and bliss.

Powerful, simple techniques, which allow us to tap into our inner resources and to enrich all areas of our lives – personal relations, physical, mental and emotional health, work and spiritual growth – are explained, so that each one of us can discover our own great potential.

Rajinder Singh is one of the world's great spiritual teachers and leaders, and his wisdom and sympathetic advice have brought spiritual benefit to thousands of people worldwide. He has also written *Vision for Spiritual Unity and Peace*, *Education for a Peaceful World*, *Ecology of the Soul* and *Inner and Outer Peace Through Meditation*.

ISBN 0 00 716149 2

Make
www.thorsonselement.com
your online sanctuary

www.thorsonselement.com

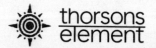

thorsons
element